COOL CAREERS WITHOUT COLLEGE FOR

MUSIC

LOVERS

COOL CAREERS WITHOUT COLLEGE FOR
MUSIC
LOVERS

**KERRY
HINTON**

The Rosen Publishing Group, Inc.
New York

T 32213

L

Published in 2002, 2007 by The Rosen Publishing Group, Inc.
29 East 21st Street, New York, NY 10010

Library of Congress Cataloging-in-Publication Data

Hinton, Kerry.
Cool careers without college for music lovers / Kerry Hinton.— 1st ed.
p. cm. — (Cool careers without college)
Includes lists of Web sites, bibliographical references, and index.
ISBN-10 1-4042-1093-8 (library binding)
ISBN-13 978-1-4042-1093-6
1. Music—Vocational guidance—Juvenile literature. [1. Music—
Vocational guidance. 2. Vocational guidance.] I. Title. II. Series.
ML3795 .H64 2002
780'.23'73—dc21

2001004184

Manufactured in the United States of America

CONTENTS

INTRODUCTION

Are you a music lover? Do you listen to your favorite music all day long and seek out new music? Perhaps you learned how to play an instrument so that you could play your favorite songs yourself. Maybe you even write and record your own music. If you are a music lover and have ever considered working in the music industry, then keep reading. This book will introduce you to many different careers within the music industry.

None of the jobs described in this book require a college degree: You can jump right in as soon as you have finished high school. As long as you have dedication and patience you can find success in some area of the music industry. While some jobs in the music business require you to play an instrument, the majority of the jobs listed in this book only require that you have a real interest in music and that you are willing to work hard to achieve your goals.

This book describes twelve different professions in the music industry. Each chapter describes a particular job; the training you will find helpful in performing the job; and places where you can find more information about the job. You will be introduced to a wide variety of careers, from selling music in a retail store to starting your own recording label. The possibilities are endless for a music lover who has the drive and determination needed to succeed in this exciting business.

RETAIL STORE EMPLOYEE

Music retail stores are a music lover's delight. Modern music stores have row upon row of different types of music: from rock and jazz to blues, country, hip-hop, and folk. Music stores offer one stop shopping for any music lover.

Music stores provide recording companies with a way to sell their products to the masses. The great thing about working in a record store is the access that employees have to a

Many bands and artists have CD release parties and signings at record stores. Store employees often have opportunities to meet successful musicians, as well as their agents and managers.

wide variety of great music. A music lover who works at such a store can sample an endless amount of new music. In addition, retail sales is a sure way to begin learning about the business side of music. Many people who work in various areas of the music industry got their start working in a music store. They gained valuable knowledge and experience before moving to another field in the music industry.

Working at a Music Store

Depending upon their size, music stores offer a variety of employment positions. Larger stores have salespeople, stockers, buyers, and managers—though some of these positions may overlap. With no experience, you'll likely start in a low level position, such as stocker or salesperson. Small stores have fewer employees, each of whom share much of the work. Starting out at a smaller store can really benefit a newcomer, as there is a greater opportunity to learn all areas of the business.

In retail sales you'll work the cash register, answer customer questions, and order out-of-stock music for customers. In addition you may find yourself stocking, cleaning, and helping the manager to open and close the store. You may also have a chance to meet and talk with representatives from record labels and promotion companies. Representatives can sometimes offer leads to employment opportunities at record labels, distribution companies, and other music-related jobs.

A higher-level retail position is that of buyer. If you enjoy music, you may find this job very appealing. As a buyer, you have a budget determined either by you, the owner, or the manager of the particular store. A buyer is responsible for using his or her budget to order the products that the store will stock and sell to the public. It is important that the buyer purchase the correct amount of each product. A buyer does not want to run out of popular items, or be left with extra product. Products include a variety of items, such as compact discs, vinyl records, audio equipment, music magazines, and blank tapes and CDs. In some cases the manager of a store also acts as buyer.

Working in a music store gives you an opportunity to explore music that you may otherwise be unfamiliar with.

Recording labels frequently contact music store managers to keep them informed of all of the most recent releases. It is up to a store buyer to determine the products that he or she will purchase for resale. Buyers make their decisions based upon sales history. This means that he or she will order products that they think their customers are most likely to purchase. Large chain stores sometimes have one buyer for a particular category of music. For instance, a person may be employed as the jazz buyer for a store. A jazz buyer will know a great deal about jazz and will know which

A record store employee checks out new music at one of the store's listening stations.

artists sell best. He or she will also keep up to date on all jazz happenings and new artists.

Managing a store in one capacity or another is usually the most senior position at a music retail outlet. Managers have much more responsibility than other employees. All employees look to the manager for direction and instruction. Managers handle customer issues and oversee the day-to-day operations of the store. At smaller, independent stores, managers do the buying as well as managing the store, and can also be responsible for duties like scheduling work shifts, signing checks, and paying bills and employee payroll.

Education and Training

A college degree is not required to work at a retail music store. Music store managers look to hire people who are sociable, hard working, and who have a real love of music. If you want to work at a retail outlet, simply apply for a job with the manager. Music stores need friendly employees who have a good base knowledge of music, and/or a real motivation to learn about it. Training is almost always on the job. Simply put, you learn as you go—by experience.

Earning a Living

Like most retail jobs, record and CD stores usually pay entry-level positions slightly more than minimum wage. According to the U.S. Department of Labor, the average hourly wage in retail is about $8.51. Employee turnover is very high in retail, so employees who seek out additional responsibilities and show that they are reliable have a good chance of moving up and receiving higher pay. At the managerial level, salaries vary by geographical location and the size of a particular business. According to the U.S. Department of Labor, the average salary for retail buyers is $40,780. Retail sale managers make on average between $22,790 and $40,100 a year.

Career Outlook

The outlook for a career as a retail store employee is above average. The U.S. Department of Labor predicts that retail jobs will increase ten to twenty percent over the next six years. Although there are fewer local music stores than in the past, there are many chain retail outlets that are always looking for employees. The popularity of deejaying has allowed the return of the old-fashioned record store, where the racks are filled with albums rather than CDs or cassettes. In addition, there are many Internet-based music retailers who still need a workforce despite the lack of face-to-face interactions with customers.

Up Close and Personal: An Interview

Ten Questions with Bronko Spaleta

Manager, Sam Goody, Hoboken, New Jersey

WHAT IS YOUR TITLE?

Store Manager.

HOW LONG HAVE YOU WORKED HERE?

I've been with the company for ten years, and at this location for one-and-a-half years.

HOW DID YOU GET THIS JOB?

Quite by accident. I was a regular shopper at a nearby Sam Goody in the late 1980s. One day, the manager asked me if I wanted a full-time cashier position. That's how it started!

DID YOU GO TO COLLEGE FOR THIS JOB?

No. I did go for media studies, but it doesn't really apply to my work here.

WHAT IS THE DOWNSIDE OF YOUR JOB?

Crazy hours! We work an uneven schedule with a lot of weekend shifts—it's our busiest time. It's also sometimes hard to manage employees who refuse to do their jobs even though they know their duties.

WHAT'S THE UPSIDE?

Free concert tickets, access to great music, and teamwork with fun employees who like music just as much as I do.

DO YOU HAVE MUCH RESPONSIBILITY?

Yes! I'm responsible for everything, even when I'm not here. If one of my employees is rude to a customer, he represents me. It's the same as my being rude to that customer. It's tough to motivate employees sometimes, too. I need their help to get work completed, even though I'm responsible for it.

DO YOU HAVE TO HIRE AND FIRE PEOPLE?

All the time. People leave for all reasons, and I couldn't tell you how many I've had to bring on board and let go over the years.

DO YOU LIKE YOUR JOB?

No.

NO?

No. I love it.

FOR MORE INFORMATION

ASSOCIATIONS

Music and Entertainment Industry Student Association (MEISA)

Web site: http://www.mnstate.edu/meisa

This is a global organization of students working with educators and music industry professionals to prepare for careers in music.

The Music Industries Association of Canada (MIAC)

33 Medhurst Road

Toronto, ON M4B 1B2

(416) 490-1871

e-mail: info@miac.net

Web site: http://www.miac.net

This is a national, nonprofit trade association representing Canadian manufacturers, wholesalers, distributors, and retailers of music-related products.

National Association of Music Merchants (NAMM)

5790 Armada Drive

Carlsbad, CA 92008

(800) 767-6266

Web site: http://www.namm.com

This organization provides everything you need to know about products for the music industry. It also includes news, information about industry events, and online courses.

WEB SITES

Billboard.com

http://www.billboard.com

This online component of *Billboard* magazine offers news, charts, trivia, and reviews.

Ice Magazine

http://www.icemagazine.com

Independent Record Store Directory

http://www.the-ird.com

This extensive online database cataloging the best and brightest of U.S. indie record stores, can even steer you to the best near you.

Internet Music Resource Guide

http://www.specialweb.com/music

This is a reference of links and other resources to Internet sites about music.

Record Store Review

http://www.recordstorereview.com

This online directory of record stores throughout the world offers reviews of customer experiences, raves, and rants.

Music Business Journal

http://www.musicjournal.org/home.html

This online music business journal was developed to increase global understanding of all issues pertaining to the music industry.

PERIODICALS

Alternative Press
Web site: http://www.altpress.com
This publication has reviews, news, and features for fans of alternative, indie, ska, electronic, dub, industrial, punk, techno, underground, rock, ambient, and experimental music.

Canadian Music Trade
Web site: http://www.canadianmusictrade.com
This publication serves Canadian music dealers and suppliers.

The Gavin Report
140 Second Street
5th Floor
San Francisco, CA 94105
(415) 495-1990
This print trade journal, along with its online component, covers the American radio industry. It also collects and compiles playlists of more than 1,300 radio stations.

Jelly
Web site: http://www.jellyroll.com
This publication features reviews of blues, jazz, country, soul, and rock.

Mojo
Web site: http://www.mojo4music.com
This British music magazine features intelligent writing that focuses on rock music.

Pollstar
4697 W. Jacquelyn Avenue
Fresno, CA 93722
(559) 271-7900
Web site: http://www.pollstar.com
A print magazine with an online component, *Pollstar* publishes concert tour schedules for music professionals.

Rolling Stone
Web site: http://www.rollingstone.com
This monthly popular culture magazine covers the entertainment industry with a special focus on music.

Spin
Web site: http://www.spin.com
The print and online versions of this magazine cover everything you'd want to know about the latest in rock music.

FOR FUN

Hornby, Nick. *High Fidelity*. New York: Riverhead Books, 1995.
This novel is about the culture of music fanatics and the record store environment. It is also a movie starring John Cusack.

Empire Records (1995)
Warner Bros.
This movie about a day in the life of young record store employees stars Liv Tyler, daughter of Aerosmith frontman Steven Tyler.

PROFESSIONAL DJ

From rocking at the radio station to beat matching at a spin-off, the world of the DJ is full of variety, opportunities, and excitement. Being a deejay, DJ, or disc jockey is yet another way to earn a living in the music industry. If you have a good-sized collection of records or compact discs, and love playing them for people, you may want to consider working as a DJ. Over the years, deejaying has evolved into an art form while also

remaining a popular form of musical entertainment at clubs, parties, and other social events.

Get into the Spin of It

Depending upon the type of music played and the venue, the setting of a DJ job can vary widely. Deejays can work in radio stations as full time employees. Sometimes they work for entertainment companies at live events such as parties and weddings. They also work for themselves—deejaying independently at special events and working as entertainment at bars and clubs. Some deejays are lucky enough to find jobs as permanent employees of dance clubs.

While some clubs provide equipment for deejays to use, a professional DJ will certainly have his or her own musical gear. The main tool of any performing DJ is a set of two devices that can play music at the same time—these are most commonly turntables or CD players. Deejays also need a mixer. A mixer is an electronic device that controls audio signals. Using a mixer allows a deejay to smoothly fade from one sound device to another. Mixers are also used to produce many different sound effects. Some CD players have a mixer

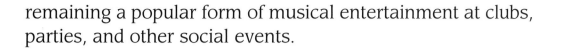

A disc jockey spins records at a backyard party.

built in. In addition to turntables and CD players, some deejays also use computers with special mixing programs.

Since he or she must perform at many different locations, a DJ's gear needs to be portable. The lighter and more compact the gear, the easier it is for a DJ to to travel to job sites. Fortunately for travelling deejays, most venues have their own sound system. A sound system is a collection of amplifiers and speakers. Amplifiers raise the level of sound from a DJ's equipment so that it can be played loudly enough to entertain an audience. Speakers project the sound.

In order for a DJ to get work, he or she needs to make a demo tape or CD. A demo is basically a DJ's audio résumé. A good demo allows a club owner or booking agent to hear a DJ's style. Once a DJ has a good demo that represents his or her abilities, the next step is to shop it around to bars and clubs. A DJ can accomplish this by giving copies to booking agents or managers at clubs who regularly book live dee-jays. If a bar or club likes the demo, they may offer performances to the DJ. If things go well a DJ may be rewarded with regular work.

Another way to earn money as a DJ is by performing at special events such as weddings and parties. Clients at special events will usually tell a DJ what kind of music they want to hear at the event. Most wedding deejays are expected to be good speakers, too. They may introduce the wedding couple and announce games or activities that are a part of the event.

If a DJ impressed the guests at an event, he or she can pick up more clients.

One initial drawback to deejaying may be age. Many places that hire DJs also serve alcohol. Depending on the state, venues may have restrictions regarding employing people under 21 years of age. However, there are still plenty of places to play, such as school dances, corporate events, and family gatherings.

Paying Your Dues

No formal training is necessary to become a DJ. The only requirements for success are dedication and practice. A DJ must spend a great deal of time perfecting his or her craft. An experienced DJ creates a sound that people enjoy listening to. A DJ needs to know how to work the equipment very well. There are a few videos out there that can teach you the basics. You can also ask your friends and family if they know a DJ personally. She or he may allow you to observe them while they work. Once you've got the basics down, you can have fun developing your own style.

Earning a Living

Many deejays only perform to supplement their incomes; others get so much work that they need managers and booking agents to keep track of their busy schedules.

High school functions, such as proms and concerts, are likely sources of work for disc jockeys.

Pay rates vary for deejays depending on the type of deejaying that they perform. According to the U.S. Department of Labor, radio disc jockeys earn between between $7.13 and $15.10 an hour. For live and event deejaying, the salary varies depending on how many bookings a DJ does each year. Pay is usually on a per-night basis and is influenced by venue size and attendance. You can check how much a DJ makes in your area by searching on the Web for DJ companies and their rates.

Career Outlook

DJ culture is very popular. Many establishments hire deejays to provide a personal and original music experience. New deejays are hired daily to add something different to the regular lineup at established dance clubs. So long as there is a demand for music in bars and clubs, there will be deejays spinning tunes for the public.

FOR MORE INFORMATION

ASSOCIATIONS

American Disc Jockey Association
1964 Wagner Street
Pasadena, CA 91107
(626) 844-3204
Web site: http://www.adja.org
This professional organization supports disc jockeys, provides them with continuing education, and offers news about the industry.

Canadian Disc Jockey Association
336 Yonge Street, Suite 141
Barrie, ON L4N 4C8
(519) 453-3136
e-mail: heckendr@cdja.org
Web site: http://www.cdja.org
This is a nonprofit trade association for disc jockeys across Canada.

Online Disc Jockey Association (ODJA)
3600 Magnolia Avenue
Reading, PA 19605
(610) 929-4315
e-mail: odja@odja.com
Web site: http://www.odja.com
ODJA promotes professionalism and maintains the highest standards in the disc jockey industry. The ODJA provides members with discounted insurance, advertising, and much more.

WEB SITES

Dusty Groove Records
http://www.dustygroove.com
Dusty Groove is an online merchant specializing in rare jazz, hip-hop, soul, and Latin music.

Groove Merchant Records
http://www.fogworld.com/gm
This is a great source for rare groove and hip-hop records.

The DJ List
http://www.thedjlist.com
TheDJList.com boasts the largest, most comprehensive source of DJ information in the world.

Pink Noise
http://pinknoises.com
An online magazine that seeks to promote the work of women deejays and sound artists.

Turntable Lab
http://www.turntablelab.com
This site is an online source for buying DJ equipment and goods.

BOOKS

Brewster, Bill, and Frank Broughton. *Last Night a DJ Saved My Life*. New York: Grove Press, 2000.
Written by two music journalists who interviewed professional DJs, music critics, industry insiders, and musicians, *Last Night a DJ Saved My Life* charts the history and examines the psychology of the disc jockey.

Broughton, Frank and Bill Brewster. *How to DJ Right: The Art and Science of Playing Records*. New York: Grove/Atlantic, Inc., 2003.
This is a handbook on deejaying.

Lindquist, Robert A. *Spinnin' 2000: The Ultimate Guide to Fun and Profit as a Mobile DJ*. E. Rochester, NY: LA Communications, 1990.
For the prospective DJ, this is a guide to making a living by playing music.

Poshardt, Ulf, and Shaun Whiteside. *Dj-Culture*. London: Quartet Books Ltd, 2000.
Poshardt focuses on the DJ's role in music history from record spinner to musician.

Reighley, Kurt B. *Looking for the Perfect Beat: The Art and Culture of the DJ*. New York: Pocket Books, 2000.
This book features interviews with real disc jockeys, chronicles the history of spinning, and also provides practical advice to the novice DJ.

Sabatke, Donald D. *Jock Itch: For Those Itching to Be a DJ*. Ixonia, WI: The Broadcasters Learning Center, 1997.
This book offers solid advice on turntable techniques for the beginner disc jockey.

Webber, Stephen. *Turntable Technique: The Art of the DJ*. Milwaukee, WI: Hal Leonard Publishing Corporation, 2000.
This is as close to a DJ textbook as you'll find. It comes with two albums to help the aspiring DJ learn how to match beats.

Zemon, Stacy. *The Mobile DJ Handbook: How to Start and Run a Profitable Mobile Disc Jockey Service*. Boston: Focal Press, 1997. This book contains valuable practical information on buying equipment, getting bookings and negotiating contracts, advertising, and other business-related tips and strategies.

PERIODICALS

DJ Times
Web site: http://www.djtimes.com
DJ Times is a trade magazine for professional deejays. This site features video interviews with top deejays, information about the industry, charts, news, and more.

DJzone
Web site: http://www.djzone.net
DJzone is the largest online network for disc jockeys. It includes articles, resources, and business advice for the professional DJ.

Mobile Beat: The DJ Magazine
Web site: http://www.mobilebeat.com
Mobile Beat is dedicated to the specialized interests of working mobile entertainers. Each issue is packed with coverage and reviews of new equipment and music along with tips on how to boost bookings and get more referrals from each performance.

The Wire
Web site: http://www.thewire.co.uk
The Wire is a monthly magazine focusing on electronica, avant rock, breakbeat jazz, modern classical, and global music.

XLR8R (pronounced "accelerator")
Web site: http://www.xlr8r.com
This monthly magazine covers electronic music and rave culture.

VIDEOS

(All available from DMC USA LTD., 133 W. 25th. Street, Suite 7W, New York, NY 10001: http://www.dmcworld.com)

The Art of Turntablism
The world's greatest deejays teach techniques.

Shure Turntablism 101
This video focuses on the philosophy of the DJ, going beyond techniques to provide the thoughts that go with the maneuvers. An all-star lineup of professional deejays break down their routines and explain the philosophy behind their moves.

So You Wanna Be a DJ?
This video shows techniques, explanations of studio technology, and interviews with top radio deejays and programmers.

3

MUSIC DISTRIBUTION

Take a look at the jacket of one of your favorite albums or CDs. On the back cover, you'll find the logo of the record company that represents the band or musician. Record companies are the core of the music industry. Record companies are responsible for the recording, promotion, and distribution of various projects from a variety of musicians and singers. Record companies have many jobs to offer to music lovers. Some record companies are small, with a few employees. Some are so large that they occupy an entire office building. The types of jobs this section will cover are jobs that you can most likely get without a college degree.

Pressing the Plastic

Every employee at a record distribution company is important to the company's end goal: getting the music to the general public. There are many entry-level positions available in the industry. One common entry-level position is working as part of a street team.

Street teams are assembled by employees of a record company. Street teams perform a number of special tasks that record company employees may not be able to perform themselves. These tasks may include hanging posters and handing out flyers and stickers. Some team members check on quantities of specific CDs at various stores in a certain area. Street team jobs are part-time and primarily intended for high school and college students. Some street team work is offered as intern work. Interns may or may not be paid for their services. Whether they are paid or not, internships offer valuable experience and often lead to full-time jobs.

Working on a street team can help you to become familiar with full-time employees at a record company. Making

A record company's mailroom is an excellent entry point into the music business. Mail clerks regularly come into contact with managers from various departments who can help them to advance their careers.

contacts with full-time employees will help you to get full-time work as positions become available. Employees who are impressed by your hard work will often recommend you for jobs.

Another common area of entry-level work is in the mailroom. The mailroom is very important part of a record company. Thousands of demo tapes and CDs of band hopefuls are sent to record companies every day. Someone needs to receive and catalog all of these demos. Record companies also receive important contracts and information through the mail. Many record companies promote entry-level employees to other jobs within the company. If you know you want to work for a record company, but you're unsure about what you actually want to do, working in the mailroom is a great start. It can give you a taste of different jobs before committing to them.

A typical promotion from an entry-level position is the job of merchandising coordinator. A merchandising coordinator's duties include overseeing street teams: making sure that they properly distribute posters, flyers, and checklists. Merchandising coordinators are given a small budget by their superiors to complete these tasks. A merchandising coordinator who knows how to stretch a tight budget is a valuable asset to the record company.

Merchandising coordinators report to product development representatives (PDRs). PDRs may be placed in charge of a certain artist or record. It's their job to publicize an artist or record so that people will buy the product. PDRs may work on one record or artist at a time, concentrating only on that project. PDRs may have several other duties to take care of as well. Being able to prioritize, meaning doing what is most important first, is a valuable PDR skill.

Paying Your Dues

No formal education is necessary for entry-level work at a recording company. Out of all of the professions in this guide, the recording industry probably has the largest number of employees who did not go to college to train for their jobs. Record companies look for tireless and enthusiastic workers. It helps to have a real love for music. Individuals who volunteer for tough assignments or harder jobs with longer hours are the employees who are usually most valued. Employers remember these employees when it is time to promote.

Earning a Living

Salaries in this line of work depend on the specific job. A person who works on a street team will usually not get paid. Most work to gain experience and make contacts that can lead to full-time work. Some perks of the job include free merchandise. Labels such as Epic advertise for street team applicants on their Web sites. Mailroom salaries are relatively low, usually starting at around $18,000 a year. By the time a person is a PDR, he or she may make around $25,000. There are also nonmonetary perks such as free concert tickets, merchandise, and the chance to meet bands and musicians.

This audience at the Concert for the Rock and Roll Hall of Fame in Cleveland, Ohio, is likely to include record company employees who got free tickets at work.

Where It Is Headed

While online downloading has taken a bite out of traditional record sales, record companies are still very much necessary. Record companies must find, foster, and represent new talent. Companies will continue to thrive and find new ways of getting music to the masses. There is a high amount of turnover at record companies, especially in lower-level positions. If one company doesn't have a need for interns, keep looking—odds are there is work to be found somewhere.

Words of Advice

When pursuing a career track in the record distribution business, it is often a good idea to start at a small company. The smaller the company, the fewer employees there are. This means that many more duties may be passed to you that wouldn't get passed to you at a big company. This will give you an opportunity to prove your skills. The most important thing to remember is to be patient. It may be a long time before you work your way up in a company, but it's well worth the time if the desire is there.

Record companies are open during the day, but musicians mostly play at night. If you think that working with record labels and artists is for you, remember that it involves working during the day and also during some of your off time. You may have to attend a concert to help ensure that a band's show runs smoothly. You may have to stay later than normal to get a large mailing together or to work on a flyer to distribute to street teams. The music industry is a busy one, especially when you work at a record company. Be prepared to remain flexible in the hours you work and the duties you perform. Also remember that the music business is always changing. If you can think of a job that hasn't been created yet, invent it yourself! Innovation is one of the hallmarks of the business.

FOR MORE INFORMATION

ASSOCIATIONS

Creative Musicians Coalition
1-24 W. Willcox Avenue
Peoria, IL 61604
(309) 685-4843
e-mail: info@amimcmc.com
Web site: http://www.aimcmc.com
This is an international organization dedicated to the advancement of new music and the success of the independent musician.

Taxi
Web site: http://www.taxi.com
(800) 458-2111
This is an independent artist and repertoire company helping unsigned bands, artists, and songwriters get deals and promotions. It is also helpful for industry listings.

WEB SITES

BMG Entertainment
http://www.bmgentertainment.com
BMG is one of the largest distributors worldwide. They represent hundreds of artists and operate all over the globe.

Independent Record Distribution Network
http://www.pan.com/indie/dist.htm
This is an online resource for distributing audio recordings that have been independently produced and released.

Internet Music Resource Guide
http://www.specialweb.com/music
This site is a reference of links and other resources to Internet sites about music.

Revolver USA
http://www.midheaven.com/revolverusa/links.html
Revolver is an independent music distributor that carries some well-known and lesser-known artists. Its eclectic roster is worth checking out, as are the FAQs about the company.

Studio K7
http://www.k7.com
Studio K7 is a fast-rising music distributor that deals mainly with electronic music. The Web site also looks cool.

BOOKS

Frascogna, Xavier M., and H. Lee Hetherington. *This Business of Artist Management.* New York: Billboard Books, 1997.
This Business of Artist Management will help anyone intending to work with musicians for a living.

Kalmar, Veronika. *Label Launch: A Guide to Independent Record Recording, Promotion, and Distribution*. New York: St. Martin's Press, 2002.
This is a how-to guide on the business, plus information on distribution.

Kashif and Gary Greenberg. *Everything You'd Better Know About the Record Industry*. Venice, CA: Brooklyn Boy Books, 1996.
This book is a comprehensive guide for anyone who wants to pursue a career in the music industry. Rapper Ice Cube calls it the new bible for the recording industry.

Krasilovsky, M. William, Sidney Shemel, and John Gross. *This Business of Music: The Definitive Guide to the Music Industry*. New York: Watson-Guptill Publishers, 2000.
This is a comprehensive reference to the economic, legal, and financial aspects of the music business. It is known as the definitive book on the music industry.

Lathrop,Tad and Jim Pettigrew. *This Business of Music Marketing & Promotion, Revised and Updated Edition*. New York: Watson-Guptill Publications, Incorporated, 2003.
This is a guide to planning and producing a complete marketing campaign for selling music to the listening public.

Passman, Donald S. *All You Need to Know About the Music Business*. New York: Simon and Schuster, 2000.
This book gives advice about negotiating deals, advisers, publishing, touring, and merchandising. It includes helpful information for anyone interested in pursuing a career in the music industry.

Schwartz, Daylle Deanna. *Start and Run Your Own Record Label*. New York: Billboard Books, 1998.
This book is especially good for beginners. Quotes from industry professionals will help those who need to know all aspects of the music business.

PERIODICALS

Billboard
1515 Broadway
New York, NY 10036
(212) 764-7300
Web site: http://www.billboard.com
Billboard is a very well-known weekly magazine dealing with the music industry. It covers all bases, such as independent music and world music and is a good place to find out who the movers and shakers are in the industry. It is available at record stores, libraries and newsstands.

The Gavin Report
140 Second Street, 5th Floor
San Francisco, CA 94105
(415) 495-1990
This print trade journal covers the American radio industry. It also collects and compiles playlists of more than 1,300 radio stations.

Pollstar
4697 W. Jacquelyn Avenue
Fresno, CA 93722
(559) 271-7900
Web site: http://www.pollstar.com
A print magazine with an online component, *Pollstar* publishes concert tour schedules for music professionals.

4

AUDIO ENGINEER

Audio engineers (also called sound technicians) are responsible for the conditioning of live and recorded music. An audio engineer who works with live music sets up a band's equipment, adjusts the sound levels of each instrument, and adds effects to the music where needed. An engineer who works in a studio setting is responsible for producing the best quality recording

An audio engineer uses a mixing board to test audio levels before a live performance.

he or she can. There are many factors that go into a good recording, such as equipment quality, and an engineer's expertise in mixing the levels of each instrument together.

Description

Simply put, audio engineers help singers and instruments to sound as good as possible. They work with sound that comes through microphones, amplifiers, or other sources, and they adjust the levels of the various sounds (the bass, drums, voice, and guitar of a band, for instance) to make them work together as a whole listening experience. Audio engineers are often called soundmen or soundwomen, because sound is the focal point of their field.

Audio engineers adjust the sounds of live and recorded performances to ensure that everyone can hear what's being said or played. They make sure the sound is as free of disturbances as possible. Disturbances refer to anything that interferes with sound quality. One example is feedback, which is the high-pitched sound that you may hear when someone talks into a microphone. Engineers also adjust the sounds to fit each performance space. They take into consideration the acoustic qualities of a room when they set up each instrument. If you look on the back of a CD or an album, the person who is credited as the "engineer" is actually an audio engineer. The producers of recorded music—CDs and records—often have audio engineer training as well.

A common tool that many audio engineers work with is called a mixing board. A mixing board is a more advanced version of the mixer that a DJ may use in a live performance. Almost any public event—political speeches, television broadcasts, live concerts—requires the services of an audio engineer.

Audio engineers are also able to perform a great number of sound-related jobs. In addition to figuring out and monitoring sound requirements, they can also repair and service sound equipment. This can range from microphones to

turntables to public address systems. Some areas of the field involve the installation of sound systems at local clubs, arenas, and radio stations. Some sound technicians work in motion pictures and commercials, inserting necessary sound effects to enhance a program. Other engineers work as sound designers, where they customize sound systems for private homes and businesses.

For larger, more complicated jobs, audio engineers often have assistants who help them with job details. For instance, checking cables and connections for the sound at a stadium would be too much work for one person. An engineer's assistants help out with such work.

Education and Training

You don't need a college degree to be a sound engineer. What you do need is a solid understanding of sound conditioning and processing equipment, such as mixing boards, amplifiers, and compressors. You also need an understanding of the nature of sound waves (or acoustics). Acoustics are the actual sound waves that an instrument produces or that a room carries. This knowledge can be gained either through

Audio engineers often take on jobs that are not directly music related. Here, members of an audio crew pack up cables for sound equipment they used for a political rally in Nashville.

working as an assistant to an engineer, or by taking audio engineering classes.

Some colleges offer sound engineering programs and classes. There are a few different pipelines to success or qualification. Check out the directory at the end of this chapter for associations that can tell you more about education opportunities in the field.

Earning a Living

According to the U.S. Department of Labor, the average salary of sound engineers is $36,970 per year. With time in the business and more responsibility, audio engineers at very high levels can demand salaries upwards of $80,000 to $100,000.

Career Outlook

The outlook for audio engineers is good. According to the U.S. Department of Labor, opportunities will increase ten to twenty percent over the next six years. Freelance work is a good way to make steady or extra income. In addition to working with music, someone with an audio engineering background will be able to find work in a variety of connected fields such as special audio effects for motion pictures and music video sound.

An audio engineer uses special equipment to test the sound system at an IMAX theater in Syracuse, New York.

Additional Information

Audio engineers often work long hours. Many engineers are also hired to tour with bands, so they are often away from home. Engineers must be flexible and learn to roll with the punches. Sometimes, despite an engineers expertise and talent, equipment just doesn't act the way it should. An engineer has to be able to weather the stress of things not going smoothly at live and studio jobs.

Mixing Consoles

A mixing console, or mixing board, is the most important tool used by an audio engineer. Indoors and out, mixing

boards allow the audience to hear a proper balance of each performer and instrument. Every microphone is plugged in to the console. The board is really like a sound laboratory; all voices and sounds come together and are processed by the mixing board (this is "mixing"). Every mixing board has a series of channels, which allow the focus to be placed on different aspects of a performance. Let's say a mixing board has sixteen channels. One of

A soundman monitors the balance of sounds at his mixing console.

those channels will be devoted just to the bass guitar. This allows an audio engineer to adjust the bass guitar's level before it goes to the speaker. The engineer can prevent it from being too loud and drowning out other instruments, or from being too quiet and unheard by an audience. Imagine fifteen more 'sounds' filling the remaining channels—the sound engineer adjusts each of them during a performance to produce a unified and pleasurable sound. Using a mixing board allows engineers to adjust bass, treble, and midrange. Mixing boards also have electronic effects, such as reverb, to enhance specific aspects of a performance.

FOR MORE INFORMATION

ASSOCIATIONS
Audio Engineering Society (AES)
60 East 42nd Street, Room 2520
New York, NY 10165-2520
(212) 661-8528
e-mail: HQ@aes.org
Web site: http://www.aes.org
The AES is the only professional society devoted exclusively to audio technology. It serves its members, the industry, and the public by stimulating and facilitating advances in the constantly changing field of audio.

Recording Industry Association of America (RIAA)
1330 Connecticut Avenue NW
Suite 300
Washington, DC 20036
(202) 775-0101
Web site: http://www.riaa.com
This trade organization represents the U.S. recording industry.

WEB SITES

Learning About Microphones
http://www.coutant.org
This online resource provides information on understanding and using microphones.

Modern Recording
http://www.fitsandstarts.com
Industry professionals share their expertise on this Web site.

Prosound News
http://www.prosoundnews.com
This site has the latest on happenings and technology in the music sound industry.

ProSoundweb.com
http://www.live-audio.com
The Live Audio Forum Board at www.live-audio.com has plenty of audio engineer resources.

The Recording Web Site
http://www.recordingwebsite.com
This site allows the user to make original music, get recording information and advice for a professional or home studio, and learn about audio production.

BOOKS

Katz, Robert A. *Mastering Audio: The Art and the Science*. Oxford, UK: Butterworth-Heinemann, 2003.
This is a handbook on recording for musicians and producers.

Massey, Howard. *Behind the Glass: Top Record Producers Tell How They Craft the Hits*. San Francisco, CA: Miller Freeman, 2000.
This book gives overviews of the creative and technical process of sound recording.

Owsinski, Bobby. *The Mastering Engineer's Handbook*. Vallejo, CA: Mix Books, 2000.
Interviews with professionals let the reader understand what the job is really about.

Owsinski, Bobby. *The Mixing Engineer's Handbook*. Emeryville, CA: Mix Books, 1999.
This text points out the key elements of mixing for beginners.

Talbot-Smith, Michael. *Audio Engineer's Reference Book*. Boston: Focal Press, 1999.
Now in its second edition, this book reflects the latest technologies in sound engineering.

White, Ira. *Audio Made Easy: (Or How to Be a Sound Engineer Without Really Trying)*. Milwaukee, WI: Hal Leonard Publishing Corporation, 1997.
This book is an introduction to live audio and recording written by a professional audio engineer who is able to relate to the layman.

Young, Clive. *Crank It Up: Live Sound Secrets of the Top Tour Engineers*. San Francisco, CA: Backbeat Books, 2004.
This book contains interviews with sound engineers who work with some of the world's biggest bands.

PERIODICALS

Audio Media
Web site: http://www.audiomedia.com
Audio Media bills itself as the world's leading professional audio technology magazine.

EQ
Web site: http://www.eqmag.com
EQ is a trade journal for serious recording professionals.

Mix
Web site:
http://industryclick.com/magazine.asp?magazineid=141&siteid=15
Mix is a trade magazine for those interested in commercial and project studio recording.

Professional Sound
Web site: http://www.professional-sound.com
This is a bimonthly trade journal for the professional sound engineer.

Tape Op
Web site: http://www.tapeop.com
This is the definitive journal of the music recording industry.

EDUCATIONAL PROGRAMS

Institute of Audio Research
64 University Place
New York, NY 10003
(212) 777-8550
Web site: http://www.audioschool.com
Located in New York City, the 600-hour Recording Engineering and Production (REP) Program offers both the in-depth technical knowledge and hands-on skills needed to begin a career in the recording industry as an assistant recording engineer or an entry-level audio technician.

Omega Recording Studios
5609 Fishers Lane
Rockville, MD 20852
(301) 230-9100
e-mail: omega@omegastudios.com
Web site: http://www.omegastudios.com
This program strives to prepare its students for the real world through instruction in the operation of recording studio, audio production, and sound reinforcement equipment. In addition, a music business curriculum is offered with the objective of preparing students for careers in the field of artist management.

The Recording Connection
(800) 295-4433
Web site: http://www.recordingconnection.com
This flexible, home-study program provides students with hands-on training in music internships in their hometowns.

5

PROFESSIONAL MUSICIAN

Some days you wish it was just you and your instrument, and the world would just melt away. You could play for hours and be lost in the moment. You've practiced a lot, and you're getting pretty good. You understand your instrument and the language of music. If you are in a situation such as this, then you might want to consider a career as a professional musician.

Job Description

If you play an instrument, your services will probably fall into one of two categories: session musician or general business musician. Session musicians work in studios or onstage. They are given a piece of music to learn and play according to the instructions of the band leader or producer of a recording session or concert. Session musicians are also know as session players, sidemen and sidewomen, or backup musicians. Session musicians are highly skilled and need to know how to read sheet music. Many write or transcribe musical notation, which is the written language used by musicians everywhere. Some truly talented individuals are able to play by ear, but it never hurts to know how to read and write notation.

Most session musicians specialize in one instrument or one type of instrument, such as stringed instruments or woodwinds. Playing more than one instrument can make you more valuable and can enable you to find work more often. For non-stage work, session musicians play at recording and sound studios. They play for movie and television soundtracks and for commercials. Session musicians also work as studio musicians for bands. Some session musicians are members of orchestras that play classical music. Orchestral jobs pay well, and offer steady work. Since they are often given music that they have never seen before and

A session musician plays his guitar during a recording session.

are asked to master it quickly, session musicians need to be easygoing and able to adapt to new situations.

Some professional musicians are known as general musicians. These musicians have learned a variety of songs, usually popular songs written by other people, from many periods of popular music. This is called their repertoire. A repertoire is like a music résumé; general musicians use their repertoire to obtain work at a variety of functions. General musicians can work alone or with a regular group

Musicians who can read and write music are likely to get more session work than those who can't.

of musicians and can play events such as weddings, birthday parties, and corporate functions. Bands that play popular, known music are called cover bands.

A professional musician can also rely on his or her voice as an instrument. Professional singers' voices have many classifications that are organized by vocal range or by style of music. The vocal ranges are soprano, contralto, tenor, and baritone. People who sing professionally also need to be able to read and write musical notation. The

human voice is an instrument that requires as much training to "play" as does, say, a cello.

Paying Your Dues

You don't need to attend music school to be a professional musician, but you have to be more than a hobbyist player. Try to learn as much as you can about musical notation and about playing your instrument. If you have some experience, the first step you may want to take is to join the band at your school or in your community, or to take private lessons outside of school. If you want to sing, join the choir or audition for a school play or musical. You can also get involved in local theatre productions.

You also don't need to attend college to be a musician. The path to success, however, includes understanding where music has been, and where it is headed. Many sessions involve a producer or director making a reference to some other song or composition. Try to study every type of music, starting with classical. Also, try to take some computer classes, because more and more sessions today involve computer software programs.

You need to be able to read music and be highly skilled at playing an instrument in order to be a member of a professional orchestra.

Earning a Living

According to the U.S. Department of Labor, the salary for singers and musicians averaged $36,290 a year. The bottom ten percent earned less than $13,040. The top ten percent earned more than $96,250. Orchestral musicians make between $734 and $1,925 weekly.

There are plenty of things that factor into how much money you can make as a musician. This includes your résumé (where you've worked before), reputation, and the hours you are available to work. Some musicians work as session musicians and general musicians at the same time. Doing multiple jobs will definitely increase what you make. Many musicians teach privately to supplement their incomes.

People who play music professionally do it because they love what they do. There is often downtime in between jobs for musicians, and many face unemployment while waiting for the next job.

Career Outlook

The environment for performing musicians is highly competitive. If this is the route you choose, make yourself as marketable as possible. Learn additional instruments and, most of all, practice. According to the U.S. Department of Labor, employment opportunities are expected to increase ten to twenty percent over the next six years. Music is always in demand and as long as it is, professional musicians will be needed.

Words of Advice

Many musicians work odd hours, which means late nights and weekends. In addition to working odd hours, professional musicians must have good social skills. Musicians have to know how to get along with other people, both in bands they may play with, and in the audience.

Location is also important. It's easier to find work as a session musician, for instance, if you live in or near a city rather than in a small town. New York, Nashville, and Los Angeles are cities that provide the most opportunities for work for professional musicians.

FOR MORE INFORMATION

ASSOCIATIONS

Creative Musicians Coalition
1024 W. Willcox Avenue
Peoria, IL 61604
(309) 685-4843
e-mail: info@aimcmc.com
Web site: http://www.aimcmc.com
The CMC is an international organization dedicated to the advancement of new music and the success of the independent musician.

Music and Entertainers Independent Student Association (MEISA)
Web site: http://www.mnstate.edu/meisa
This is a global organization of students working with educators and professionals from the music industry to prepare for careers in music.

WEB SITES

Canadian Musician
http://www.canadianmusician.com
Canadian Musician is a print magazine, but its Web site also has some material from past issues, including networking information for musicians to meet one another.

Carol Kaye's Web Site
http://www.carolkaye.com.
Carol Kaye is the First Lady of the bass guitar, an instrument not many women are famous for playing. She has great advice for musicians and her story is interesting to read. She actually became a session player by accident!

Electronic Musician
http://www.emusician.com
This is a Web resource for recording professionals.

Internet Music Resource Guide
http://www.specialweb.com/music
The Internet Music resource Guide links to Internet sites that are music resources.

Sonic State
http://www.sonicstate.com
Sonic State links to music resources on the Internet.

BOOKS

Coryat, Karl. *Guerrilla Home Recording: How to Get Great Sound from Any Studio*. San Francisco, CA: Backbeat Books, 2004.
This text offers information on how to record in any studio.

DeSantis, Jayce. *How to Run a Recording Session*. Emeryville, CA: Mix Books, 1997.
It's best to know what to expect when you enter the recording studio and this book includes information on studio engineering.

Halloran, Mark. *The Musician's Business and Legal Guide*. Upper Saddle River, NJ: Prentice Hall, 2001.
Twenty-two entertainment lawyers break down legalese into language everyone can understand.

Kashif and Gary Greenberg. *Everything You'd Better Know About the Record Industry*. Venice, CA: Brooklyn Boy Books, 1996.
This is a comprehensive guide for anyone who wants to pursue a career in the music industry. Rapper Ice Cube calls it the new recording industry bible.

Krasilovsky, M. William, Sidney Shemel, and John Gross. *This Business of Music: The Definitive Guide to the Music Industry*. New York: Watson-Guptill Publishers, 2000.

This is a comprehensive reference to the economic, legal, and financial aspects of the music business. It's known as the definitive book on the music industry.

Lathrop, Tad, and Jim Pettigrew. *This Business of Music Marketing and Promotion*. New York: Billboard Books, 1999.
This is a guide to planning and producing a complete marketing campaign for selling music to the listening public.

Passman, Donald S. *All You Need to Know About the Music Business*. New York: Simon and Schuster, 2000.
This book gives advice about negotiating deals, advisers, publishing, touring, and merchandising. It includes helpful information for anyone interested in pursuing a career in the music industry.

Perry, Megan. *Wired: Musicians' Home Studios: Tools and Techniques of the Musical Mavericks*. San Francisco, CA: Backbeat Books, 2004.
Offers an in-depth look at recording from a performer's perspective.

Rapaport, Diane Sward. *How to Make and Sell Your Own Recording*. Upper Saddle River, NJ: Prentice Hall, 1999.
This book gives guidance on recording, pricing product, and selling your recordings via the Internet.

Schulenberg, Richard. *Legal Aspects of the Record Industry: An Insider's View*. New York: Billboard Books, 1999.
Here's an overview of all things legal with regards to the music industry. It includes annotated examples of contracts.

Spellman, Peter. *The Self-Promoting Musician: Strategies for Independent Music Success*. Boston: Berklee Press Publications, 2000.
This book gives valuable guidance about adding all-important business expertise to artistic talent when pursuing a career as a musician.

Stim, Richard. *Music Law: How to Run Your Band's Business*. Berkeley, CA: Nolo Press, 2001.
Here's helpful advice from a musician and an attorney about the legal side of music.

6

MUSIC BROADCASTER

When you tune into your favorite radio station, the sound that you hear is an audio signal. Many people are involved in producing this invisible signal and in getting the signal to you. Music broadcasters work together to create and broadcast the programs that you hear on the radio. There are many opportunities to work in music broadcasting, such as radio and Internet stations.

Announcers are the people whose voices you hear on a radio broadcast. They are sometimes known as radio personalities or deejays. These deejays are different than the ones described in chapter two. Announcers introduce news, weather, interview segments, guests, and music. Most deejays on the air don't get to pick the material they play. Instead, they are given a playlist that is made by a programming director. The programming director decides what a station will play, based on the station's format, or music type. There are many different formats on the radio. Turn on your radio and turn the dial—every type of music is represented, from country to rock to hip-hop to dance. Some smaller radio stations and Internet music sites are free-form, which means they may not play only one sort of music. These are great places to work if you want to learn about a large range of music types.

Music directors keep a station's music catalog, or library, up-to-date. This is an ongoing job as new recordings are constantly being released by record companies. The playlist of a station is always changing, which can be both exciting and frustrating at the same time. Every week, the programming director and music director (sometimes it's the same person) decide which songs to drop or add from the station's playlist.

Despite their popularity with the listening public, most radio deejays have little influence on the radio station's playlist.

Another important job in broadcasting is that of sound engineer. People who listen to the radio want what they hear to sound good, just like concertgoers or people who buy a new record. It takes more than one sound engineer to make a station run. Often a station will have a chief sound engineer who works with a few assistant sound engineers. The chief engineer is responsible for all of the technical aspects of a radio broadcast. They are responsible for making sure that the sound signal leaving a radio station is of the highest possible quality.

Radio stations also need people to write material for the deejays, research listener information, maintain the station's electronic equipment, and sell advertising time to businesses who want to promote their products. They need mail clerks, office assistants, and interns, too. There are many different entry-level opportunities at radio stations.

Paying Your Dues

You can find entry-level work at a radio station even without a college degree. From there, a person with drive, a good work ethic, and a can-do attitude can find opportunities for promotion to more senior-level positions. People with computer skills are at an advantage here, as more and more radio outfits are becoming increasingly digital and computerized. Take advantage of computer programs that your school may offer. After school, you may want to invest in some basic broadcasting courses at a local technical school to get a better understanding of the technical side of the industry. There are also broadcasting schools that offer one- or two-year programs in all aspects of the business.

Without a bachelor's degree in broadcasting, it is a little more difficult to break into the announcing side of radio. Experience is as important as a college degree in some aspects of the radio business, so try to obtain as much as possible while you're still in school. If you want to be an on-air personality, get involved in activities at your school that are related, such as the school plays, debate team, or announcing for the football or the basketball teams.

See if there are any small, locally run stations and ask to intern. Some radio stations at colleges need volunteers or interns to help out in the off months when students are away. You may not be getting paid, but it is free training. Use this opportunity to get involved early; while others are studying about broadcasting, you'll be learning first hand. When they're ready to enter the work force, you'll already have experience. The more motivation you display as an intern, the more you increase your chances of getting hired for a full time paying job.

Earning a Living

If you're interning to gain on-the-job training, you're most likely not getting paid. Some internships may offer a stipend.

Radio deejays must often stick to a playlist set by their program directors.

This is a small amount of money to cover little expenses. Hang in there; this is definitely a profession that requires experience before you can rely on it as a steady source of income.

According to the U.S. Department of labor, the average salary of broadcast techs is $27,760. Radio sound engineers make about $36,970. The average hourly wage of an announcer is $9.91.

Where It Is Headed

According to the U.S. Department of Labor, job openings in broadcasting other than announcing are expected to increase ten to twenty percent over the next six years. The popularity of Web radio stations has added to the places where you will be able to apply. The job of an announcer is really coveted, so practice your chops and get ready to spin some tunes.

FOR MORE INFORMATION

ASSOCIATIONS AND PLACES OF INTEREST
Museum of Television and Radio

In New York:
25 West 52nd Street
New York, NY 10019
(212) 621-6600
Web site: http://www.mtr.org

In Los Angeles:
465 North Beverly Drive
Beverly Hills, CA 90210
(310) 786-1025
Web site: http://www.mtr.org
This museum—one branch in Los Angeles, the other in New York City—collects and preserves radio programs and makes them available to the public. The museum also puts together interesting exhibitions.

National Association of Broadcasters (NAB)
1771 N Street NW
Washington, DC 20036
(202) 429-5300
e-mail: nab@nab.org
Web site: http://www.nab.org
This is a full-service trade association that promotes and protects the interests of radio and television broadcasters around the world.

WEB SITES

BE Radio
http://www.beradio.com
This is a full-service online industry magazine with excellent editorials, features, news, issues, product reviews, and other important information regarding the radio industry.

Inside Radio
http://www.insideradio.com
This online magazine is updated frequently and has the latest on what's happening on the business side of the radio industry. It also looks at important people in the business. Overall, this is a good starting point to learn some terms and facts about commercial radio.

Radio Locator
http://www.radio-locator.com
This is a search engine that allows you to search for any radio station broadcasting in the United States by music type. You can also search for

any station broadcasting music over the Internet worldwide. Did you ever wonder what's big in Bolivia or France? Check out this site.

Radio Online
http://www.radioonline.com
Radio Online covers news, trends, ratings, and everything else you can think of in the radio industry. It also posts job openings around the country.

Ruffsounds.com
http://www.ruffsounds.com
Designed specifically for radio talent, this site helps radio broadcasters find the information they need for their shows, such as news, entertainment and music happenings, humor, and sound bites.

BOOKS

Staff, Mike. *How to Become a Radio DJ: A Guide to Breaking and Entering.* Troy, MI: Happy Communications, 1998.
This book suggests strategies for breaking into the world of radio deejaying. Check out www.djbook.com for information.

Wolfgang, Larry D. Now You're Talking!: All You Need to Get Your First Ham Radio License. Newington, CT: American Radio Relay League, Incorporated, 2003.
This book is a guide to setting up your own short-wave radio broadcast.

EDUCATION/TRAINING

Noncollege broadcast schools are available throughout the United States and Canada. Here are a few correspondence programs that offer distance-learning courses, local internships, and apprenticeships.

Air Time Radio Broadcasting School
(800) 345-2344
Web site: http://www.broadcasting-school.com
This school offers a comprehensive list of courses relating to radio broadcasting and placement in internships all over the country.

Broadcast School in a Box
Web site: http://www.broadcastschool.com
This is a program that you can do at home, even while holding another job. Students are hooked up with internships in their area, because experience is the best way to get a job in radio broadcasting. Check out the Web site for testimonials from people who have benefited from this program.

Get a Mentor—Apprentice Mentor Association
Web site: http://www.getamentor.com
This organization sets up its students with apprenticeships in the radio business. The idea is that working closely with a mentor will teach the student more than he or she would learn in a classroom, and also that he or she would be a more attractive candidate for future jobs, having had the benefit of a mentor.

FOR FUN

Airheads **(1994)**
20th Century Fox
Brendan Fraser and Steve Buscemi play two band members who really (really) understand the wide audience you can reach via the radio waves.

FM **(1978)**
Universal Studios Home Video
Somewhat dated, but a good look at the bad side of the radio industry.

Pump Up the Volume **(1990)**
New Line Cinema
Christian Slater stars in this movie about a high school kid who starts a pirate radio station in his basement.

7

INSTRUMENT TECHNICIAN

When you're watching your favorite band rock out live, you're not just watching them work. You're witnessing a complex system of sound, and behind the scenes, people are making that work, too. These "invisible" bandmates are known as instrument technicians. They're often nicknamed "roadies," and they are the backbone of musical

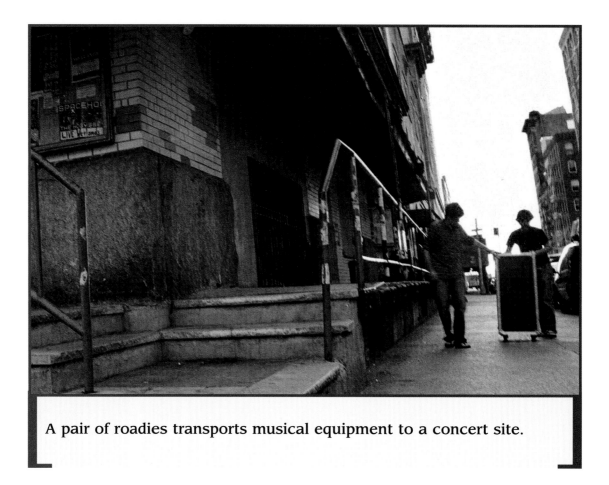

A pair of roadies transports musical equipment to a concert site.

and theatrical companies. They travel all over the world to help bring entertainment to the public.

Check, Check, One, Two, Three . . .

Roadies have training and expertise in areas connected with live performances, such as lighting, stage design, instruments, and sound (see audio engineer). Instrument technicians also support touring musical groups in surprising ways. They take care of costumes and food. They drive the band bus and the trucks containing equipment. Depending on the size of the operation, a crew of instrument technicians can range from two men who are responsible for all of the technical support to hundreds of members.

If you decide to become a roadie, you are really becoming a kind of performer. Singers can't be heard if the microphones and speakers don't work, and they can't be seen if the spotlights are burnt out or aimed wrong. Instrument technicians perform, but they do their performance where no one in the audience can see them. If you can play an instrument well, but are not interested in being the person in front of the crowd, you may want to try being an instrument technician. A few shows are so big, that each instrument has its own technician. There are plenty of jobs that help shows or performances run, so you could see which ones interest you most.

Instrument technicians obtain work on a local or regional level, as well as on a national level. Local work is close to home and involves helping out local bands or providing technical support for the community theater group. Check local papers and music magazines to see who may need help in your area. The regional level is more involved. First, it involves traveling, which is one way to see another part of the country while you work. Regional tech crews are usually small, consisting of two to three people. They assist bands or touring companies of shows, such as a Broadway

A young instrument technician monitors the sound and lights before a nightclub performance.

hit. Working at the regional level usually requires experience, which can be gained locally. Occasionally, however, regional companies will take on apprentices to train. The national level (sometimes international, too) is where the most skilled and experienced technicians find work. At this stage, the level of technical skill is very high, and the chances of being away for long periods of time is even higher. Some jobs can even involve several months of travel in another country.

One of the keys to being an instrument technician is dedication. It may take some time to progress from working locally to working nationally, but persistence pays off. The more you work at a local or a regional level, the more people you will meet who may be able to help you find work with a traveling company. Your résumé of experience may be on paper, but your reputation is built by putting on good shows. Sound systems that provide thrilling, live entertainment are remembered by people who hire and rehire techs.

Another important key is your ability to get along with people under stressful situations. Traveling and working with a bunch of people for a prolonged period of time means that a roadie has to be able to work well with other people. Everyone who works for a band or on the crew of a touring show should have the same goal: the best performance possible every time.

Paying Your Dues

You won't need a college degree to get hired as a roadie. That doesn't mean you've got it easy. You will eventually have to prove your worth on the road and under stressful, important conditions.

You can see if it's for you by starting in high school. Work as a stagehand for a school or local production. You'll learn the basics and find out where your talent lies. You also can contact the local branch of the International Alliance of Theatrical Stage Employees (IATSE), or a professional sound and lighting company and ask to intern for them.

Earning a Living

The pay varies for each level of work, as well as for particular jobs; some bands or companies may pay more than others. At the regional level, techs usually get paid per gig, so the work may only be part-time. As roadies move to higher levels of responsibility the pay will increase, and so will the hours. According to RoadCrews Touring Ltd, unskilled roadies earn around $25,000 a year. Techs with a lot of skill or experience earn $60,000 or more.

FOR MORE INFORMATION

ASSOCIATIONS

The International Alliance of Theatrical Stage Employees (IATSE)
Moving Picture Technicians, Artists and Allied Crafts
1515 Broadway
Suite 601
New York, NY 10036
(212) 730-1770
Web site: http://www.iatse-intl.org
According to its site, the IATSE is "the labor union representing technicians, artisans and craftspersons in the entertainment industry, including live theatre, film and television production, and trade shows."

WEB SITES

Applause Music Careers
http://www.cnvi.com/applause
This Web site is a great resource of any aspect of the industry, but has an especially good section on instrument technicians.

Backstage World
http://www.backstageworld.com.
Backstage World is another Web site dedicated to support staff.

Pro Lights and Staging
http://www.plsn.com
News, reviews, interviews, features, and behind-the-scenes info.

Roadie.net
http://www.roadie.net
A companion to Karl Kuenning's book, *Roadie: A True Story*, this Web site tells you everything you want to know about the life of a roadie, including job details, news, gig postings, advice on breaking into the business, roadie lingo, and message boards.

Roadogz
http://www.roadogz.com
Billed as "survival for the people on the road in the entertainment industry," this Web site posts articles, editorials, stories, product reviews, message boards, and even games and travel information—anything of interest to people working on the technical side of the entertainment business.

RoadCrews Touring Ltd.
http://www.roadcrewstouring.com
An online resource offering information and interviews with some of the top roadies of today.

Rock the Roadie
http://www.rocktheroadie.com
Created by a veteran roadie, this Web site serves as an advertisement for *The Roadie Guidebook,* the practical manual for anyone who dreams of following their favorite band around the world.

Stagespecs.com
http://www.stagespecs.com
This site has job postings, industry news, important links, and all kinds of resources for theatrical and stage professionals.

Tour Support.net
http://www.toursupport.net
This Web site is the self-described "Online Home of Touring Professionals." It offers weather forecasts, games, and tips for those who earn their living on the road. Check out the message board for job openings.

BOOKS

Kuenning, Karl. *Roadie: A True Story (At Least The Parts I Remember).* New York: Writer's Showcase, 2001.
This is a true account of the trials and tribulations of a traveling roadie/instrument technician from the 1970s to the 1980s.

Melnick, Monte A. and Frank Meyer. *On The Road With The Ramones.* London, UK: Sanctuary Publishing, 2003.
This book offers the perspective of a head roadie who spent years working for the Ramones.

Reid, Francis. *The ABC of Stage Technology.* London: A & C Black, 1995.
This text provides basic information about working on the stage.

8

BOOKING AGENT/CLUB MANAGER

There is a thrill and excitement to a live show that you just can't get from an album. Music fans go to clubs, bars, and stadiums to see bands perform live. Musicians tour to reach the fans personally, and to make more income. A lot of planning goes into bookings and tours. If you're great at organizing, you could be the person

A club manager surfs the Web while the club is closed. In a few hours, the bar will be packed with people and the band will be jamming.

who sets up the tour or booking; the booking agent or club manager.

Come to Our Show

Club managers take care of the day-to-day details of keeping a venue open and letting people hear live music. The list of responsibilities is long: Hiring and paying employees, paying bills, and keeping inventory of refreshments are just a few. A manager's job is to manage all of the resources he or she has to help things run as smoothly as possible on any given night of the week. Managers of places that serve food and alcohol have to deal with special licensing and city laws. Most businesses are licensed by a city or a state; there are dozens of types of licenses. Many cities even require a license for clubs to allow dancing. These licenses insure that the building is safe for the stress that a floor full of dancers can cause. If you manage a club, you'll have to maintain a budget. Businesses can only spend as much money as they make, and everything costs money, from licenses to payrolls to heating bills.

Booking agents at live venues are in charge of booking, or scheduling, live music. Booking shows can be difficult. In larger cities, there can be competition among clubs to book certain artists who are very likely to draw large crowds. This means the band will want more money. Like club managers, booking agents also need budgeting skills. Musicians can't play a venue if the money earned isn't enough to cover their own costs (such as gas, instrument repairs, and backup singers). If a booking agent, also called a booker, books a show and is unable to pay a band because of the club's costs (like paying staff and sound engineers), his or her reputation could be damaged. Over time, this results in decreased ability to attract bands with higher profiles.

In some clubs, the manager and the booker are the same person. This is a huge responsibility, but it also keeps everything under the control of one person, which can

Booking agents schedule talent at theaters, universities, music venues, and comedy clubs.

eliminate possible conflicts. For example, if one person books shows and another person manages, misunderstandings could be more likely to happen about dates, times, needed equipment, and who is actually booked.

In addition to clubs that specifically feature music, bookers and club managers can also find employment opportunities at local theaters, comedy or variety clubs, and private and public colleges and universities. Musicians may not be the only type of entertainment, but the experience can lead to a job dealing specifically with musical bookings.

Paying Your Dues

You don't need a college degree to be a booker or manager. Some community colleges and local institutions offer small business courses, but they aren't specifically suited to this job. What you will need is drive and experience. Many people in this field start at entry level, performing smaller tasks to help with the overall running of a club or a venue.

Any job related to the venue can provide you with valuable experience; it takes more than one person to help a show or a concert run smoothly. The club manager or booker needs people to take tickets, watch the door, and promote shows, to name just a few duties.

Like most really interesting and challenging jobs involving music, you have to work your way up by taking jobs that in themselves might not seem exciting. They will, however, give you experience, allow you to watch how things work, and let you see how certain decisions affect the outcome of a particular problem or situation. This is valuable knowledge for a successful booker or manager.

Earning a Living

The salaries of booking agents and club managers vary, depending on a few things. One is venue size: Bigger places hold more people and sell more tickets. Another is reputation: Clubs with credibility can draw more popular acts. Many managers and bookers get a set salary and are sometimes rewarded with a small percentage, or commission, of the total profit resulting from a particular performance.

Where It Is Headed

Live performances will never go out of style. The U.S. Department of Labor expects a job growth of ten to twenty percent over the next six years for musicians, which translates to about the same for the people who schedule their performances.

Music at Maxwell's: Personal Interview

Ten Questions with Todd Abramson
Owner/Booking Agent, Maxwell's, Hoboken, New Jersey

HOW DID YOU GET INVOLVED WITH LIVE MUSIC?
Well, I started coordinating live shows when I was in high school. I'd have local bands play in my basement when my parents went away for the weekend. When I moved east, I had a friend in New York who was a musician and suggested I try my hand booking shows part-time at a club called Folk City.

HOW LONG HAVE YOU BEEN AT YOUR CURRENT JOB?
On and off for fifteen years. The original owner sold the bar, and I had the chance to buy it with some other investors a

few years ago. I've been booking shows since I've worked here, though.

WHAT DO YOU THINK IS THE KEY TO SUCCESS IN YOUR LINE OF WORK?

Mainly, exude calm at all times. If you have a crisis, freaking out about it will only make matters worse. Remember that somebody has to keep a clear head.

IS IT HARD TO BE BOTH BOOKER AND MANAGER?

Sometimes it is, but in tough situations, the booker and manager have to support one another and not argue or have conflicts, so I guess in that respect, it's easier to do both jobs.

DO YOU HAVE MUCH FINANCIAL RESPONSIBILITY?

Yes!!! My partner helps out, but I usually handle the day-to-day stuff like budgets and salaries.

WHAT IS YOUR ADVICE TO SOMEONE WHO WOULD LIKE TO DO WHAT YOU DO?

Start early. Get involved, stick around, and show people you're dependable. Employers reward good employees, and they really reward good employees they can trust. Be a self-starter.

WHAT'S THE BEST WAY TO GET BOOKING CONNECTIONS?

First, go to shows. If you see a band you like, talk to them and start to develop a relationship. If they live far away, e-mail them. It's easier to network now than it was when I started. Most bands have a Web site, too. Use that to your advantage—be aggressive!

WHAT IF YOU'RE UNDER TWENTY-ONE?
That can be an obstacle, but there are still places that put on shows for people under the drinking age. We do shows like that here sometimes. The connections may be fewer, but the same rules apply.

IS YOUR JOB CHALLENGING?
Sometimes. Angry road managers, staffing problems, and unruly crowds are tough enough alone, but when they all happen together, that's when it's challenging.

DO YOU LIKE YOUR JOB?
I wouldn't be doing it otherwise.

FOR MORE INFORMATION

WEB SITES

Internet Music Resource Guide
http://www.specialweb.com/music
This is a reference of links and other resources to Internet sites about music.

Taxi

http://www.taxi.com

(800) 458-2111

This is the site for an independent artists and repertoire company helping unsigned bands, artists, and songwriters get deals and promotions. It is also helpful for industry listings.

BOOKS

Colby, Paul and Martin Fitzpatrick. *The Bitter End: Hanging out at America's Nightclub.* Lanham, MD: Rowman & Littlefield Publishers, Inc., 2002.
This book offers a behind-the-scenes look and history of the rise of a club under the management of its manager-turned-owner.

Frascogna, Xavier M., and H. Lee Hetherington. *This Business of Artist Management.* New York: Billboard Books, 1997.
This text will help anyone intending to work with musicians for a living.

Kashif and Gary Greenberg. *Everything You'd Better Know About the Record Industry.* Venice, CA: Brooklyn Boy Books, 1996.
This is a comprehensive guide for anyone who wants to pursue a career in the music industry. Rapper Ice Cube calls it the new bible for the recording industry.

Krasilovsky, M. William, Sidney Shemel, and John Gross. *This Business of Music: The Definitive Guide to the Music Industry.* New York: Watson-Guptill Publishers, 2000.
This is a comprehensive reference to the economic, legal, and financial aspects of the music business. It's known as the definitive book on the music industry.

Passman, Donald S. *All You Need to Know About the Music Business.* New York: Simon and Schuster, 2000.
This book gives advice about negotiating deals, advisers, publishing, touring, and merchandising. It includes helpful information for anyone interested in pursuing a career in the music industry.

Stiernberg, John. *Succeeding in Music: A Business Handbook for Performers, Songwriters, Agents, Managers and Promoters.* San Francisco, CA: Backbeat Books, 2002.
This is an introduction to the various careers in music and how to succeed at them. It also includes interviews and a CD.

PERIODICALS

Alternative Press
Web site: http://www.altpress.com
Alternative Press features reviews, news, and features for fans of alternative and experimental music.

Pollstar
4697 W. Jacquelyn Avenue
Fresno, CA 93722
(559) 271-7900
Web site: http://www.pollstar.com
A print magazine with an online component, *Pollstar* publishes concert tour schedules for music professionals.

9

MUSIC PROMOTER

Do you ever ask your friends to listen to the music that you like? Do you tell others about upcoming albums or news about musicians? If so, you may have the knack for promoting music for a living. The world of music is so big that most people don't have the time to keep up with new artists, new CDs, new singles, and news. The music promoter keeps up with all this for the general public.

Sorting Through a Mountain of Music

Promotion companies are independent companies that work with record labels, management, and artists to increase public knowledge of a particular song, record, album, or musician. This work is known as publicity. People who work in publicity make their client or project as public and well-known as possible.

There are many levels of promotion. Some promotions take place on a grassroots level, meaning they are local yet very effective. You may have seen posters around your town or city that advertise musicians or albums. A grassroots publicity team probably put them there. The posters did their job, because you saw them. A big national advertising company didn't put them there; a small local group did.

A farther level of publicity is accomplished by using the Internet. The Internet reaches all distances; from the massive public in a big city to the farmer in a rural community. Promotion companies use the Internet and e-mail to inform people of upcoming tours, recordings, and general news involving their clients.

Big promotion companies may work directly with a record label to develop a general marketing strategy to

Street teams are responsible for the promotional posters often seen on scaffolding boards and in store windows.

publicize a musical act. Bigger labels have more money to use to promote their artists. They can take out television and radio ads, whereas a local artist with limited funds cannot.

Music promotion companies use merchandise to make their client and their client's music more memorable. Merchandise ranges from stickers with a band logo to an added value gift to encourage people to buy an artist's album. Some companies reach individual communities by doing things locally, like painting a car with the name and picture of a musician and displaying it at malls. Some arrange contests that coincide with tour dates in local markets. Winners receive free merchandise or tickets while the word on the band is being spread by the contest itself.

Many promotion companies use a combination of approaches when it comes to publicity—the Internet, e-mail, patches, stickers, as well as the old-fashioned approach of calling record stores, radio stations, and DJs. Promoters must be tireless, and exhaust every avenue they can think of to get public notice. Even though this is the computer age, many people still like personal interactions with one another; many businesses try to combine the old and the new to take promotions into the twenty-first century.

Paying Your Dues

A candidate with enthusiasm and fresh ideas is just as important as a candidate with a college degree. Experience

Janet Jackson greets fans outside a New York music store as she arrives for an in-store promotion of her album, *Velvet Rope*.

and previous knowledge of promotions will also help you succeed in landing a job. As with most jobs in the music business, there aren't any academic programs that specifically teach music promotions. However, many community colleges offer marketing courses, which provide a solid background in the principles behind promotion. A sure way to become involved with music publicity is to intern part-time to gain some knowledge about the general goings-on until a paid position opens up. Many people who work in publicity have worked at record labels or stores, where they

Make Room for Dessert

Rawkus Records, a New York City–based rap and hip-hop label, completely understands the importance of using as many resources as possible to spread the word on the street about their label and their clients. During warmer months, Rawkus employees cruise the avenues and streets of New York in a hand-painted ice-cream truck! They actually serve ice cream. The truck carries the names of rappers on the label, especially those with new albums that are about to be released. The driver also carries special promotional materials for anyone who'd like to find out more about Rawkus clients.

There is huge potential for this promotion to gain more recognition for Rawkus artists— someone may never have heard a single record the label puts out, but one thing is certain: Everybody likes ice cream. Combining certain types of music with other consumable promotions is not new, but the people at Rawkus managed a new twist on the formula.

had an introduction to promotion. Some people even decide to branch out and start their own promotion companies after they have learned the basics from a larger company.

Earning a Living

Salary depends on the promotion company and its size. A company with many clients will pay more, but will probably require you to work longer hours. The pressure could be much greater than at a smaller firm. Part of your salary may also depend on your personal ability to attract and produce results for certain clients. Employers keep track of the successful publicity campaigns, and the employees who spearheaded them. Successful campaigns lead to promotions and more earnings. This type of job falls under the category of promotions specialist. According to the U.S. Department of Labor, the average salary for a promotions specialist is $41,710 per year. Annual salaries range between $24,240, and $75,100 depending on individual circumstances. Perks include free concerts and merchandise, and being ahead of the breaking news in music.

Where It Is Headed

According to the U.S. Department of Labor, employment of promotion specialists is expected to increase twenty-one to thirty-five percent over the next six years. The outlook depends on the music industry itself. So long as there are records to promote, there will be a need for promoters.

FOR MORE INFORMATION

WEB SITES

Girlie Action
http://www.girlieaction.com
This is the site for a New York City–based public relations and marketing business.

Holiday Matinee
http://www.holidaymatinee.com
This is the site for some music promoters based in San Diego.

Internet Music Resource Guide
http://www.specialweb.com/music
This is a reference of links and other resources to Internet sites about music.

Melting Vinyl
http://www.meltingvinyl.co.uk
Melting Vinyl is an English company that promotes all kinds of music. Check out their site to learn about the work involved.

BOOKS

Frascogna, Xavier M., and H. Lee Hetherington. *This Business of Artist Management.* New York: Billboard Books, 1997.
This text will help anyone intending to work with musicians for a living.

Kashif and Gary Greenberg. *Everything You'd Better Know About the Record Industry.* Venice, CA: Brooklyn Boy Books, 1996.
This is a comprehensive guide for anyone who wants to pursue a career in the music industry. Rapper Ice Cube calls it the new bible for the recording industry.

Krasilovsky, M. William, Sidney Shemel, and John Gross. *This Business of Music: The Definitive Guide to the Music Industry.* New York: Watson-Guptill Publishers, 2000.
This is a comprehensive reference to the economic, legal, and financial aspects of the music business. It's known as the definitive book on the music industry.

Lathrop, Tad, and Jim Pettigrew. *This Business of Music Marketing and Promotion.* New York: Billboard Books, 1999.
This is a guide to planning and producing a complete marketing campaign for selling music to the listening public.

Passman, Donald S. *All You Need to Know About the Music Business.* New York: Simon and Schuster, 2000.
This book offers advice about negotiating deals, advisers, publishing, touring, and merchandising. It offers helpful information for anyone interested in pursuing a career in the music industry.

Pettigrew, Jim. *The Billboard Guide to Music Publicity.* New York: Watson-Guptill Publishers, 1997.
The Billboard Guide to Music Publicity informs the reader about how to create press kits and other ways to get the word out about a musician or a band.

Stiernberg, John. *Succeeding in Music: A Business Handbook for Performers, Songwriters, Agents, Managers and Promoters*. San Francisco, CA: Backbeat Books, 2002.
This is a guide to the business side of music.

PERIODICALS

Alternative Press
Web site: http://www.altpress.com
Alternative Press features reviews, news, and features for fans of alternative, indie, ska, electronic, dub, industrial, punk, techno, underground, rock, ambient, and experimental music.

Billboard
1515 Broadway
New York, NY 10036
(212) 764-7300
Web site: http://www.billboard.com
Billboard is a very well-known weekly magazine dealing with the music industry. It covers all bases, such as independent music and world music.

Pollstar
4697 W. Jacquelyn Avenue
Fresno, CA 93722
(559) 271-7900
Web site: http://www.pollstar.com
A print magazine with an online component, *Pollstar* publishes concert tour schedules for music professionals.

10

INSTRUMENT MAINTENANCE AND REPAIR

Nothing wrecks a musician's day (or night) more than an instrument that won't play. When the tuning goes out, a great song goes bad. Instruments are a musician's tool for expression, and sometimes those tools need fixing. That's when a certain music specialist saves the day; the instrument repairer goes to work.

Tune in to the Details

Music repair and tuning requires incredible skill and training, probably more skill and training than many of the jobs described in this book. People who perform this work usually specialize in a particular type of instrument, rather than attempt to repair every instrument under the sun. People who want their pianos tuned don't call tuba repairers—they call an expert on pianos.

There are four major types of instruments that people repair: piano/organ, band, violin, and guitar. Although guitars and violins both have strings, they are very different in many other ways. Special attention is needed for each type of musical instrument because each type has its own dynamics. What caused a guitar to go out of tune won't be the same cause of a drum going out of tune.

You may see a simple stuck or broken key on a piano's keyboard, but what the repairer and tuner sees is the thousands (yes, thousands) of parts that make up the average piano. If you were to look inside a piano, you would see dozens of strings. To tune a piano, each string has to be adjusted individually. This usually takes about two hours on the average.

Piano repair and tuning is a painstaking process. The repairer needs to know not only the relationships between keys and strings, but also the proper sound of each key.

Band instruments are those instruments played by traditional orchestras, rather than those used by a rock band with guitars and amplifiers. Band instruments include brass and wind instruments, as well as percussion instruments. Brass and wind instruments use the musician's breath to make sound. They include tubas, trumpets, trombones, oboes, cornets, French horns, flugelhorns, saxophones, contrabasoons . . . The list could go on for a long, long time.

In order to know what's wrong with an instrument, a repairer needs to know how to play that instrument. Repairers and tuners also perform the important task of cleaning musical equipment. Brass and wind instruments have many moving parts that could stick or prevent air from passing through them correctly if dirt and dust were allowed to collect.

Percussion instruments are instruments that have skin stretched over a frame and are tapped to make sounds. Snare drums, congas, tympani, and bongos all fall into this category. Repair persons may have to cut and stretch a new skin over a snare drum, adjust its tension, or repair cracks in cymbals.

Violin tuners tune and repair violins and other stringed instruments that are played with a bow. These instruments

A repairman examines an out-of-tune cello. Like all instrument tuners, he can play the instruments he works on.

include cellos and violas. Many musicians love to keep their violins for a long time. The repairer and tuner needs a delicate but capable touch.

Guitar tuners and repairers work on electric and acoustic guitars, as well as bass guitars and other stringed instruments. A common repair is replacing the frets on the neck of the guitar. A repairer needs a skilled understanding of frets as well as a skilled hand for tiny, precise work.

In addition to the main categories, there are other instruments that require special and singular attention, such as pipe and electronic organs, and electronic instruments such as keyboards and drum kits.

Musical instrument repairers and tuners often work alone. They work in a quiet environment in order to tune instruments precisely. Tuners and repairers work in a variety of locales, including repair shops and music stores. Piano tuners often travel to do their work, since the instruments are difficult to move.

Paying Your Dues

Instruments have a monetary and emotional value. Musicians don't leave them in the hands of someone unless they trust that person's ability. Many repairers and tuners began by training under others. This is called an apprenticeship, which is like interning. A good way to get in at this level is to show up already knowing a great deal about the instrument. Read repair and tuning books and watch videos. Practice on a broken instrument.

Music instrument stores are another place to look. You may begin there as a trainee. A trainee might sell sheet music or stock inventory while he or she is learning the ropes of repair under an expert. On the average, training in this way can take anywhere from two to five years.

Success will come easier if you take classes. Many community colleges and music schools offer courses in instrument repair and tuning. Instrument repair schools offer training, lasting as long as one or two years of study.

Earning a Living

According to the U.S. Department of Labor, repairpersons and tuners earn an hourly wage ranging from $7.50 to $30.68. The majority of repairpersons and tuners make about $14.15 an hour.

Where It Is Headed

According to the U.S. Department of Labor, opportunities in the repair and tuning industry are expected in increase three to nine percent over the next six years. This is even more of a reason to get involved at an earlier age if you feel like this is an avenue of employment that you may want to pursue. Since training takes some time, job openings come and go at a slower rate than that of other professions. The more training and knowledge a person has will make him or her all the more valuable in the next few years.

FOR MORE INFORMATION

ASSOCIATIONS

Musical Instrument Technicians Association (MITA)
(800) 942-7870
e-mail: info@mitatechs.com
Web site: http://www.mitatechs.com
MITA is an association of worldwide professional technicians organized to improve the electronic music service industry.

National Association of Professional Band Instrument Repair Technicians (NAPBIRT)
P.O. Box 51
Normal, IL 61761
(309) 452-4257
e-mail: napbirt@napbirt.org
Web site: http://www.napbirt.org
This is the association for band instrument repairers. NAPBIRT is a valuable resource for news and information regarding instrument repair and also training and apprenticeship opportunities for learning the craft.

Piano Technicians Guild (PTG)
3930 Washington Street
Kansas City, MO 64111-2963

(816) 753-7747
e-mail: ptg@ptg.org
Web site: http://www.ptg.org
PTG is a nonprofit association of piano technicians. The organization publishes the monthly Piano Technicians Journal and holds events and seminars for piano tuners and repairers.

WEB SITES

David T. Van Zandt
http://www.vanzandtviolins.com
David T. Van Zandt is a Seattle violin maker. His Web site lends insight into the world of someone who completely loves his work.

Instrument Repair Stuff
http://www.instrumentrepairstuff.com
This site is dedicated to supplying the repairer with the tools necessary to do the best job possible.

Precision Instrument and Equipment Repairers @ U.S. Department of Labor
http://stats.bls.gov/oco/ocos199.htm
This is an online resource listing the details of the career.

BOOKS

Barclay, Robert. *Preservation and Use of Historic Musical Instruments.* London, UK: Earthscan/James & James, 2004.
This guide explains how to preserve valuable historic instruments.

Brosnac, Donald. *Guitar Electronics for Musicians*. New York: Amsco Publications, 1983.
Guitar Electronics for Musicians will tell you everything you want to know about maintaining your electric guitar.

Burton, Stanley. *Instrument Repair for the Music Teacher*. New York: Alfred Publishing Company, 1978.
This book is a practical and comprehensive text on instrument repairs that commonly challenge the music teacher.

Cumpiano, William R., and Johnathan D. Natelson. *Guitarmaking Tradition and Technology: A Complete Reference for the Design and Construction of the Steel-String Folk Guitar and the Classical Guitar.* Amherst, MA: Rosewood Press, 1987.
This book includes all of the details you need to know to build your own classical or steel-stringed guitar. Information on suppliers, dimensions, and materials is indispensable.

Erlewine, Dan. *Guitar Player Repair Guide.* San Francisco, CA: GPI Books, 1990.
Guitar Player Repair Guide is a step-by-step manual to maintaining and repairing electric and acoustic guitars and basses. The book covers new tools and techniques, and provides detailed information on adjustments and repairs for specific models and manufacturers.

Faust, Oliver C. *The Pipe Organ and Player Piano—Construction, Repair, and Tuning.* Los Angeles, CA: Wexford College Press, 2003.
This guide explains the dynamics of organs and pianos.

Fillet, Pieter J. *D.I.Y. Guitar Repair.* New York: Music Sales Corporation, 1984.
This is an invaluable manual for every guitarist. Diagrams and photos teach the reader how to carry out dozens of repairs including fixing loose frets, dealing with a warped neck, the correct way to put on new steel strings, adjusting the bridge, adjusting a guitar for lefthanded users, and more.

Hopkin, Bart. *Musical Instrument Design: Practical Information for Instrument Making.* Tuscon, AZ: See Sharp Press, 1996.
This book gives a comprehensive overview of design principles for acoustical instruments with detailed illustrations.

McKeen, Patrick L. *Keep Your Gear Running: Electronics for Musicians.* New York: Schirmer, G., Incorporated, 2004.
This book explains the electronic elements of instruments.

Meyer, Raymond F. *Band Director's Guide to Instrument Repair*. New York: Alfred Publishing Company, 1973.
This is a practical guide with complete information on repairing band instruments right in the classroom.

Reblitz, Arthur A. *Piano Servicing, Tuning, and Rebuilding*. Vestal, NY: Vestal Press, 1993.
This is the ultimate reference book and instruction manual for both the professional and the amateur. This book examines different styles of pianos and their parts and clearly instructs the reader in evaluating; cleaning and doing minor repairs; regulating; tuning theory and procedure; and complete restoration.

Wake, Harry Sebastian. *Violin Bow Rehair and Repair*. San Diego, CA: Harry S. Wake Publishing, 1997.
One of the best and easiest to understand manuals on the subject of rehairing, repairing, and restoring bows, this clearly written text is supplemented with eighty-eight photographs and drawings.

11

MUSIC JOURNALIST

The world of music doesn't exist on its own. The public has a keen interest in favorite bands and musicians. People love taking a peek at the scenes and lives behind the music. This is where the music journalist can be found. He or she is digging up facts, news, and information on the music-makers of today.

Music journalists strive to present fair and accurate stories. Music journalism jobs are not easy to get; they are relatively glamorous. Competition to be paid to meet popular musicians, see their shows, and talk to them about their records can be intense. If you have the drive to be on the go and the persistence to work in a competitive market, this may be a job to further explore.

Hot Off The Presses

The majority of music journalists (also called music critics, rock critics, and music writers) perform a similar task— writing about music. Some music writers review new records and CDs. The articles they write, called reviews, tell the public whether or not they should buy the album. New records are released every week, so reviewers never run out of subjects. Record reviewers have to have opinions, but must be open to review all kinds of music, not just their favorites.

Interviews are a big part of publicity for new albums. People like to hear what their favorite artists have to say outside of the songs. Via e-mail, telephone, or armed with a tape recorder, interviewers talk to the music-makers and try to put an interesting spin on the story. They try to report something quirky or different, as many writers may be writing about that artist at the same time.

The movie *Almost Famous* is the story of a young music journalist who follows a band on tour. In the scene above, the legendary Lester Bangs (Philip Seymour Hoffman) gives advice to a novice writer (Patrick Fugit).

Paying Your Dues

You don't need a college degree to write about music. Many applicants with a degree in journalism may be favored over a writer with no prior experience, so the thing to do is gain experience. People who write about music have to be very knowledgeable about all types of music. Being able to write well is also a requirement. Community colleges and local writing workshops offer courses in writing, which can be very helpful in polishing your communication skills.

You can start training on your own in high school. If your school has a newspaper, see if there are any openings that involve music writing. If your school doesn't offer a paper, try writing for a local arts paper or a newsletter. Take any writing jobs you have a chance to during this phase of your development. This will also give you a sizable portfolio. A portfolio is a collection of your best work. You'll use it as a sample to show prospective editors and employers. Magazines and e-zines (online magazines) don't hire without an idea of a person's writing skill and style.

You can also use the Web to stock your portfolio. Almost every site related to music has a section that reviews records and CDs. Many don't pay. Online music stores post reviews from customers, and that can be a good place to start. Write your own reviews and submit them. Then print them out when they are posted. The idea is to have a collection of clips (published writing samples) to show to a potential employer. Take a look at the major music magazines at the local bookstore or magazine stand, and familiarize yourself with the kinds of records that get reviewed. Examine the way in which they are reviewed. Figure out the writing style, and whether you get a good sense of the music being reviewed through the writing.

Earning a Living

The salary of music writers is largely freelance. This means writers get paid an agreed-upon sum of money before they

Journalists interview rhythm and blues legends Fats Domino *(left)* and Ray Charles *(right)* at a restaurant.

write a piece. The sum is usually paid by the word and can vary. Experienced writers get higher sums per word. Some magazines and Web sites pay per review. Some writers will take a job for a small sum in the hopes that they will earn more money as they continue to write for and develop a relationship with a particular publication.

Words of Advice

Music writing is a very competitive field. You should expect it to be slightly harder than in some of the other jobs we've discussed. As long as people continue to listen to music, writers will be there in some capacity to talk about it. If you are not writing for anyone and don't have a portfolio or writing samples, write reviews of records you like or feel strongly about, and send them to various publications. You won't always receive replies about your submissions. Be prepared to have your writing rejected sometimes. The more you write, the better your work will be, and the better your chances of being published.

FOR MORE INFORMATION

WEB SITES

Music-Critic.com
http://www.music-critic.com
Check out these online reviews of the latest in rock, pop, electronica, urban, jazz, classical, and country releases and see if you can do better.

Music-Critic.ca
http://www.music-critic.ca/v3
This example of an online music review resource has interviews and "reviews worth listening to."

MusicJournalist.com
http://www.amwp.org
This site has tips and resources specifically for music writers and photographers. It includes industry directories; news, features, and articles; and mailing lists.

BOOKS

Bangs, Lester. *Psychotic Reactions and Carburetor Dung*. New York: Vintage Books, 1998.
A collection of Lester Bangs's writing from the early 1970s up until his death in 1982.

DeRogatis, Jim. *Let It Blurt*. New York: Broadway Books, 2000.
Let It Blurt is the biography of Lester Bangs, the man who changed the face of music criticism forever. His story is sad, funny, and moving. The included rare essay entitled "How To Be A Music Critic" is just as memorable.

Fong-Torres, Ben, and Cameron Crowe. *Not Fade Away: A Backstage Pass to 20 Years of Rock & Roll*. San Francisco, CA: Backbeat Books, 1999.
This book features interviews with and editorials about musicians from a renowned critic.

Meltzer, Richard. *The Aesthetics of Rock*. New York: De Capo Paperbacks, 1987.
In this book, Meltzer, a music writer, explores the music scene "on the edge" from 1966 to 1968.

PERIODICALS

MOJO
Web site: http://www.mojo4music.com
MOJO is an expensive British magazine but has some of the best writing about music on the planet. Go to a bookstore and leaf through a copy— it's like reading the history of rock, R & B, and rap in every issue.

Pollstar
4697 W. Jacquelyn Avenue
Fresno, CA 93722
(559) 271-7900
Web site: http://www.pollstar.com
A print magazine with an online component, *Pollstar* publishes concert tour schedules for music professionals.

Rolling Stone
Web site: http://www.rollingstone.com
A bimonthly popular culture magazine, *Rolling Stone* covers the entertainment industry with a special focus on music.

Spin
Web site: http://www.spin.com
The print and online versions of this magazine cover everything you'd want to know about the latest in rock music.

Vibe
Web site: http://www.vibe.com
Great writing covering hip-hop and R & B music can be found in *Vibe*.

FOR FUN

Almost Famous (2000)
DreamWorks SKG
A teenager gets his first gig writing about a band and following them on tour in this movie starring Kate Hudson and Billy Crudup.

12

STARTING YOUR OWN RECORD LABEL

Have you ever liked a band before they became popular? Have you ever heard a song that you knew would become a hit, and you were proven right? You may have the ear—and mind—of an independent label owner. If you have the knack of knowing great music, you may want to think about going into business for yourself! You don't need a million dollars, or even a thousand—only a desire to succeed and the will to work for a really demanding employer: you.

Ownership 411

In the world of record labels, there are usually a few big fish, many middle-sized, and even more smaller ones. The big labels have products you'd most likely see in larger stores, hear on the radio, or see on video a few times in any given day. These companies have enough money to promote many acts in many places at one time. They have the resources to push a band or musician until the public takes to it. Many big labels are part of larger corporations, which tie many labels together. Smaller labels are known as independents. Many independent labels are made of regular young men and women who love music and are trying to follow their own musical vision.

The first step in starting your label is acquiring some funds. You don't need a lot of money, just enough to cover the basic expenses, like producing and pressing the music you want to represent. You'll also need to legally protect the company name. You'll want to own the rights to your company's name so no one else can use your brand name to sell their records.

Your record label, now named, will need talent to represent. If you're a musician, you could also be one of your own

Indie folk-rock queen Ani DiFranco records on her own label, Righteous Babe Records, which allows her to produce music without interference from studio executives.

acts. Otherwise, you'll need to scout for talent. You can't sign someone who already has a contract, so you'll have to hunt for people just like yourself: independents. Most musicians who aren't session musicians or who work at their craft part-time will be like you. They'll know they must start small, and won't expect a million dollar contract from you.

A great way to find talent is by asking friends who are in bands or by going to local performances. Legwork pays off. Attending as many local shows and concerts as you can will give you a good idea of the talent pool in your area and

If you want to sign bands to your label, you should attend local shows to discover new talent. Unsigned bands play frequently at local clubs.

will help you determine what kind of music you want to represent on your label.

As the head of a label, your job is also to take care of the day-to-day details concerning the label's talent. Depending on the size of your company (remember to start small), the needs will not be incredibly demanding, but they'll keep you busy and require you to be organized and dedicated.

The key to organizing and running your label is using computers. Doing business online can be your best friend. You can e-mail people who have signed your band's mailing

Working online can help those who start their own record label compete with the big leaguers. Close contact with fans and potential fans can be accomplished through a professional Web site and e-mail distribution.

list at a show and let them know what the band is doing. This is also a great chance to let them know about any other recordings your label may have to offer. You can send out breaking news such as new signings, or unscheduled or short notice shows. Hopefully, they will pass the word on to their friends. You can also build a Web site for your label to show who your talent is and to reach the public.

Paying Your Dues

You don't need a degree to run your own label. You do need a good understanding of the business, which can be learned by interning at a label before starting your own. The fundamental aspects of record labels are incredibly similar, despite the number of clients on your roster, the number of your employees, or the audience you reach.

As mentioned earlier in this book, start small and start soon. Computer experience will make this and many of the professions listed in this book easier. There are employers out there who won't hire people without some computer experience or knowledge. Knowing about computers, the Web, and music software will also help your label stay ahead of the times. It's also a relatively inexpensive way to reach a very broad public.

Where It Is Headed

Large record labels are flooded with demos from bands hoping to be the next big thing. Often times, a band will receive representation, and release an album that won't produce expected sales. That band is usually passed over by the next band in line. This makes small labels appealing to many bands. Small labels invest more time and energy into representing a band, which means a more personal effort than at a big label.

FOR MORE INFORMATION

WEB SITES

Ace Fu Records
http://www.acefu.com
This is an example of an independent label.

My Pal God Records
http://www.mypalgodrecords.com
Like Ace Fu Records, this label was started by ordinary people with very little money. Both Web sites have a section that tells a little about the difficult process of starting a record label.

DIYsearch
http://www.diysearch.com
This search engine (DIY stands for "do it yourself") is a nonprofit cataloguing resource for independent artists, focusing on the arts, music, and humanities communities.

Independent Record Distribution Network
http://www.pan.com/indie/dist.htm
This is an online resource for distributing audio recordings that have been independently produced and released.

Internet Music Resource Guide
http://www.specialweb.com/music
This is a reference of links and other resources to Internet sites about music.

Music Biz Academy
http://www.musicbizacademy.com
A Web site for independent musicians and businesspersons for selling, promoting, and doing music on the Web.

Soundclick.com
http://www.soundclick.com
This site features signed and unsigned bands. Labels can upload MP3s of their artists to the site.

BOOKS

Brabec, Jeffrey and Todd Brabec. *Music, Money, and Success: The Insider's Guide to Making Money in the Music Industry*. New York: Schirmer Trade Books, 2004.
This comprehensive guide is for anyone interested in the music business.
Frascogna Xavier M., and H. Lee Hetherington. *This Business of Artist Management*. New York: Billboard Books, 1997.
This Business of Artist Management will help anyone intending to work with musicians for a living.

Kashif and Gary Greenberg. *Everything You'd Better Know About the Record Industry*. Venice, CA: Brooklyn Boy Books, 1996.
This is a comprehensive guide for anyone who wants to pursue a career in the music industry. Rapper Ice Cube calls it the new bible for the recording industry.

Kalmar, Veronika. *Label Launch: A Guide to Independent Record Recording, Promotion, and Distribution*. New York: St. Martin's Press, 2002.
This is a how-to guide on launching your own label.

Krasilovsky, M. William, Sidney Shemel, and John Gross. *This Business of Music: The Definitive Guide to the Music Industry*. New York: Watson-Guptill Publishers, 2000.
This is a comprehensive reference to the economic, legal, and financial aspects of the music business. It's known as the definitive book on the music industry.

Lathrop, Tad, and Jim Pettigrew. *This Business of Music Marketing and Promotion*. New York: Billboard Books, 1999.
This is a guide to planning and producing a complete marketing campaign for selling music to the listening public.

Passman, Donald S. *All You Need to Know About the Music Business.* New York: Simon and Schuster, 2000.
This book gives advice about negotiating deals, advisers, publishing, touring, and merchandising. It includes helpful information for anyone interested in pursuing a career in the music industry.

Schulenberg, Richard. *Legal Aspects of the Record Industry: An Insider's View.* New York: Billboard Books, 1999.
This is an overview of all things legal with regards to the music industry. It includes annotated examples of contracts.

Schwartz, Daylle Deanna. *Start and Run Your Own Record Label.* New York: Watson-Guptill Publications, Incorporated, 2003.
This book is especially useful for beginners. Quotes from industry professionals will help those who need to know all aspects of the music business.

Sweeney, Tim, and Mark Geller. *Tim Sweeney's Guide to Releasing Independent Records.* Torrance, CA: T.S.A. Books, 1996.
This book teaches the reader how to set up his or her own independent label, produce records, get distribution into major retail outlets, design a promotional strategy, and get records played on the radio.

GLOSSARY

book To schedule a band or an artist to play live music in a venue.

clips Published writing samples.

commission Percentage of the profit earned by a performance, an artist, or a recording.

distro Short for "distribution."

DIY Do it yourself.

feedback High-pitched output that often occurs when someone speaks into a microphone.

format Type of music a radio station plays.

free-form Radio station that plays music across all genres and doesn't stick to one format.

guerrilla promotions Local, grassroots form of promotion involving street teams.

indie Shorthand for independent; in the music business, it refers to performers or labels who are "small" and don't have a large amount of financial support.

mixing board or **mixer** Equipment used by a DJ or a sound engineer that combines and adjusts sounds from different sources.

mom and pop Term used to describe labels and music stores that are run by a few individuals, rather than by a large conglomerate.

music notation Written language of music.

playlist List of songs that the music director of a radio station has determined will be played by the station's disc jockeys.

portfolio Collection of an applicant's work (usually writing samples or art pieces) that serves as a sort of résumé.

promo Short for "promotional." Promos are usually free CDs given to writers, distributors, and music stores to promote a piece of music that is scheduled for an upcoming release.

repertoire Group of songs that a singer or a musician is prepared to perform.

residency Regular, long-term gig for a band or DJ to perform in a venue.

roadie Also known as an instrument technician. Prepares the set for a musician, a band, or a show by tuning the instruments, checking the sound, and doing other tasks that contribute to the success of a production.

stipend An allowance for expenses, such as living, entertainment, travel, or meals.

street team Group of unpaid people hired by a record company to promote a musician or a band at the street level.

INDEX

About the Author

Kerry Hinton is a freelance writer who lives in Hoboken, New Jersey. He has spent the past six years working in and writing about the music industry. He currently manages a record store.

Photo Credits

Cover © Eliane/Corbis; p. 9 © Willie Hill Jr./The Image Works; p. 10 © Katy Winn/Corbis; p. 12 © Tomas del Amo/Index Stock Imagery; p. 13 © Grantpix/Index Stock Imagery; pp. 21, 22 © S.I.N./Corbis; p. 26 © Arlean Collins/The Image Works; p. 32 © James Keyser/TimePix; p. 34 © Tim Hall/Getty Images; p. 37 © Tony Dejak/AP Wide World Photos; pp. 43, 50 © Ghislain and Marie David de Lossy/The Image Bank; p. 44 © Jacques M. Cherret/Corbis; p. 46 © Mark Humphrey/AP Wide World Photos; p. 49 © Syracuse Newspapers/The Image Works; pp. 56, 58 © Tom Sistak/*The (Ottawa) Daily Times*/AP Wide World Photos; p. 59 © Bill Varie/Corbis; p. 60 © SuperStock; pp. 67, 69 © Larry Lawfer/Index Stock Imagery; p. 72 © Grantpix/Index Stock Imagery, Inc.; pp. 77, 78 © Tina Fineberg/AP Wide World Photos; p. 80 © Michael S. Yamashita/Corbis; pp. 85, 86 © Bob Daemmrich/The Image Works; p. 88 © Reuters NewMedia Inc./Corbis; pp. 95 and 96 by Cindy Reiman; p. 99 © Ed Bailey/AP Wide World Photos; pp. 105, 106 © Gianni

Design and Layout

Evelyn Horovicz